Courtesy of Christian Treber, www.ctreber.com

Te Puia O Whakaari
(White Island)

A Journey Through Fear to Confidence

In Toxic Air,
On Trembling Soil

The Story of a 1960 Expedition to White Island (Te Puia O Whakaari), New Zealand's Most Active Volcano

Ray W. Lincoln

A Journey Through Fear to Confidence

ISBN (paperback): 978-0-9835718-1-0
ISBN (ebook): 978-0-9835718-2-7

Library of Congress Control Number: 2011916971
Printed in the United States of America

Apex Publications
Littleton, CO USA

Contents

Te Puia O Whakaari
(White Island)

Many people (I'm one of them), feel that an adventure is to be experience three times: in your imagination as you plan and prepare for it, in real time as you live it, and in your memory as you recall the significant events that positively affected you the most. This expedition provided all three — in spades. Entering the mouth of an active volcano *while it is a state of partial* eruption requires planning, provides and impactful experience and produces vivid memories. Those memories may be positive or negative, and which we choose to remember will determine the affect the experience has on us.

Travel with me via a verbal view of our destination and its dangers.

White Island has been an active volcano for 150,000 years, according to scientists. The volcano is made of rhyolite (the lava form of granite, which is typically very acidic and contains quartz) and andesite (a very dark mineral). It poses a threat to the mainland Bay of Plenty area of New Zealand, and official statements informing residents of its possible behavior have, from time to time, been issued.

Geologic History

It is thought that White Island was created by the subduction of the Pacific Plate under the Australian Plate. Apparently, a conduit to the surface was created over a hot spot in the earth's crust. The hot spot is called a *magma chamber*, which is the power source for a volcano, generating the heat by chemical reactions that give volcanoes their awesome power.

White Island's very large magma chamber is estimated to be many cubic miles in size. This is the reason the volcano has been able to stay active and belch gas, ash, and steam almost continually, without running out of energy, for such a long time. Scientists conclude it has been active in this way for 100,000 years or more. Frequent, more major volcanic eruptions have also occurred to punctuate its constant gas and ash emissions.

Pyroclastic Eruptions

When groundwater saturates the crater floor, it weakens its structure, and the crust of the crater floor collapses into the eruption conduit (the vent) and falls on top of the magma chamber miles below. The magma chamber doesn't like this, so to speak, and spits all the mess out. The result is a violent ash, steam, and gas explosion, which can come at any moment and without warning, generating a high-velocity column of gas and ash that can rise to a height of a little over three miles above the volcano.

These eruptions are particularly dangerous because they can produce pyroclastic flows over the crater floor and beyond.

Note: A pyroclast is a small fragment of detrital volcanic material that is aerially expelled from a volcano. Detrital material is degenerating or disintegrating rock.

This pyroclastic material is carried up with the eruption column, high above the crater floor, and when the column becomes too dense to remain buoyant, it collapses and rains hot ash and gas down on the crater at great speed, racing outward across its floor like a gaseous tidal wave to the crater's edges or beyond. This covers the floor of the crater with a white ash and obliterates all its spectacular colors. Pyroclastic flows are an imminent threat and will instantly kill anybody caught in their path. Dr. Marian Bland commented to me that, from her own infrared experience, even an airplane flying through a pyroclastic cloud will get glass shards stuck in the engines, which is what happens when the volcanic ash rises up high enough into the atmosphere.

Gasses and Thermal Activity

Gasses made up of steam, carbon dioxide, sulphur dioxide, and some halogen gases at a temperatures above 800 degrees centigrade are ejected from all the fumaroles and the main vent, forming acid droplets in the steam. These gases are severely damaging to cameras, electronic equipment, and clothing, not to mention skin and lungs. If your eyes start stinging from a sudden drift of gas, you must close them immediately and lie or crouch down. Walking with eyes closed can result in falling into one of the dozens of vents, only to be immediately cooked by the gases and hot liquids, let alone marinated by the acids. Just the thought should be enough to keep you from wandering about with your eyes closed.

The crater floor is extremely hot, as you can imagine, and if it were not for the almost constant cool ocean breezes, it would be impossible to explore the island. The heat varies according to the activity in the volcano's conduit, but is always extreme. The rising and falling of the magma is what causes the variation in temperature.

Four hundred tons (800,000 pounds) of sulphur dioxide each day is ejected, requiring the degassing and cooling of what is estimated to be several tens of cubic miles of magma over the last 16,000 years that the island is deemed to have been as active as we see it today.

The crater is also the seat of considerable hydrothermal activity with hot springs, fumaroles, geysers, steam vents, and explosive craters within an extensive crater floor measuring about one half mile by one quarter mile. We were witnesses to all these hydrothermal formations.

Size

Seventy percent of the volcano is under water, making it a massive volcano — one of New Zealand's largest, if not the largest. It was built in alternating layers of ash and lava flow, and it slopes from a wide base to the comparatively narrow top in which the crater is housed, and that is what we see above sea level.

White Island is a submerged stratovolcano (the term refers to the way it is formed) about 30 miles off the coast of New Zealand. The island is 1.2 miles in diameter at sea level, rises 1,053 feet above sea level with crater walls of 1,015 feet high. The main vent is only 38 feet above sea level and, therefore, poses the possibility of blowing itself out to sea level, which would create a steam-blast eruption — the worst kind of volcanic explosion and one that would devastate parts of the mainland of New Zealand. "No worries, mate, it hasn't done so yet," as the Kiwis say!

Monitoring

We visited the crater in 1960 when no monitoring was being done. From 1976 (when monitoring was seriously undertaken) to 1993, the volcano experienced its most active recent period. Monitoring is not only in the interests of science but the welfare of the thousands of residents on New Zealand who could be adversely affected by a tsunami.

Currently, two web cameras in the crater plus one at Whakatane, one seismograph, and a microphone have been installed. A visit is performed every 4-6 weeks, if possible, by scientists to obtain leveling measurements for detecting the rising or falling of the crater floor (the crater floor typically rises before an eruption) and to check temperatures to help detect eruptions and the movement of the magma up and down the vent. A close watch is kept on earthquakes and the movement of the Pacific and Australian plates as well.

Potentiality

When the Island erupts, ash, highly acidic gas, lava bombs — some as large as houses — pumice, and pyroclastic material are ejected. A large eruption, of which the volcano is capable, could produce a tsunami that would wipe out two cities and other towns on the Bay of Plenty coastline.

The Roll of the Reverends

Of interest and known to the author is that the first account of the crater's appearance was given by the fearless Rev. William Sewell, M.A., who went ashore while traveling nearby on a ship.   Another reverend explored it in 1960.

The Expedition

It was 1960 when I led an expedition to White Island, New Zealand's most active volcano. Named for its light grayish appearance and called in Maori, "Te Puia o Whakaari" (The Dramatic Volcano — whakaari originally meant "rude exposure"), it is of great interest to scientists and tourists, posing a fascinating sight from Whakatane, the nearest city.   Flights in helicopters are available to view the island and give tourists an up-close but safer exposure to this intriguing volcano at the southern end of the Pacific trough that is named after the island.

We were able to land by boat in quiet swells at Crater Bay and explore the entire crater from one end to the other and one side to the other. The exploration of the crater took about five hours plus time to disembark the party and reembark them, one-at-a-time, by way of a small dinghy. Most of the party stayed in and around Crater Bay, being ill equipped and (some) unwilling to explore the crater.   Perhaps they possessed wisdom! The island was in partial eruption at the time, belching a column of gas and ash some three to four thousand feet into the air from the main vent.   Other vents were vibrating and spewing toxic material, but none was observed to be ejecting lava bombs.

More vents than we could count were active, and it was tricky to avoid the clouds of gas as we traveled the half mile to the crater's back wall, examining all interesting sites as we went. The walls were almost vertical and the air currents, powered by ocean breezes and the rising heat within the crater, seemed to be circling and then escaping upward and over the 1000-foot walls — tricky, but ideal conditions for exploration of the crater floor.

The Island has been active almost continuously with severe eruptions on an irregular schedule but quite frequent. The last major eruption was in 2004, and boats are currently being warned to stay away as there have been almost 60 earthquakes in the region in the last 3 months. Indications are that it will blow again soon in a more major way. Other notable eruptions, some pyroclastic in nature, were recorded in 1914, 1960, 1976-1993, 2000, and 2004. In 1914, ten to twelve people who were on the island were killed and their sulfur mining facilities were destroyed. Their bodies have never been found. No attempts at inhabiting the island for any purpose have since been tried.

Eruptions have ejected lava flows, volcanic mud, scoria rock (which has been hurled for miles), pyroclastic materials, plumes of ash that belch several thousand feet high, and gaseous clouds that are highly acidic and deadly to life. While in even minor eruptions (like the ones we experienced), the floor of the crater trembles and toxic, acidic gases are only avoided if the air currents inside the high crater walls are favorable. The purer air is under the clouds of rising or swirling gases.

The crater floor has changed many times after major eruptions: from a crater floor containing a large lake of acid, to smaller lakes whose levels rise and fall, to streams of acid with hundreds of sulphuric fumaroles, silica formations, plus boiling mud pools and small gas vents scattered all over the crater walls to a height of about three hundred feet. At times, more than one major vent has opened up simultaneously in the crater floor.

Within a day or two of our arrival and unknown to us (cameras and devices that now monitor the volcano's behavior had not yet been installed), the island had erupted, again in some unknown fashion, and the back wall of the crater, "rotten" from so many active vents, had collapsed, creating a 300-foot high ledge that nearly smothered the main vent. This ledge also had active vents all over it.

The crater featured a large vent that covered at least one quarter of an acre, and another main vent (about 50 feet across and 50 feet deep) acted strangely, vibrating and spewing gases while its floor leapt up 12 feet or more every minute and then subsided, threatening to be the next problem vortex. The slope leading up the edge of this hole was slippery volcanic mud. More than one main vent has, at times, been seen on the crater floor.

While we gathered the information we needed and traveled over the entire crater floor, the main vent continued to belch toxic gasses and ash in the form of a solid volcanic column and roared at a deafening volume, displaying a power that would make a jet engine seem like a toy.

The crater floor was covered in fumaroles and fantastic, delicate silica formations stained with the minerals ejected from the earth's crust. Reds, oranges, yellows, browns, greens, and even some blue formations were striking and beautiful. In delta-like formation, shallow streams of acid, one to three inches deep, filtered their way down to Crater Bay, dissolving the stitches on the soles of our boots and causing us a minor change of plans.

The acid laden air also dissolved any garment of cotton or nylon, which caused a second temporary retreat to dress in rubberized boots (called gumboots) and oilskins. It emphasized the need to keep under the clouds of gas so that our lungs and our skin would not burn so acutely and our clothes would remain intact.

A party of 15, made up of support personnel and a base leader, remained on the boat or close to Crater Bay and away from the gases. I (as leader) along with one of the photographers made up an advance party of two and penetrated the crater to the back wall behind the main vent, reporting on all its features and finally climbing the 300-foot ledge that had been created by the eruption that occurred shortly before our visit.   Two others also traveled halfway into the crater to remain in sight of the advance party and relay supplies and information as needed.   Together with a geologist, who studied the formations and reported on geological features, all 20 of us made our own personal history that day. The sights, sounds, and feelings remain vivid.   Even the fear we encountered can be easily recalled, although as I will explain, we choose not to recall it. After all these years, our victory over personal fear serves as a welcome reminder of the fear-management tactics we learned.

Since the expedition was dangerous and tested everyone's courage, it can serve as an instructive model to show how we can overcome fear and build confidence, even in the most difficult circumstances in our daily lives. All of us need these lessons, whatever the intensity of our fears, since one of the greatest battles we face in life is keeping fear under control and managing its effects. A side benefit, when I did overcome my fear, was that I was introduced to a world of beauty and color that I had not seen before, nor have I seen since.

The "inside story" of fear and confidence, as experienced that summer day under a blue sky and with the island putting on a frightening exhibition of its power, tested the following lessons learned in the preparation months and exercised during our adventure into the volcano. This account is not meant to be a complete map of how to battle fear, but serves as a practical guide and trustworthy model for all the significant daily fears we might face, as well as the intense ones.

These lessons, which are not new, have been with us for ages and utilize our knowledge of how we have been created, a knowledge that is expanding with every new confirmation or discovery of science. We are reminded repeatedly how resourceful and resilient humans are who, as some of us believe, have been created in the image of God.

How to Overcome Fear and Build Confidence

Preparations

Are humans a bundle of fears? At times we believe that is an obvious truth. It isn't. We can all be courageous, and this book is about making the change from being a bundle of fears to being confident and capable. It is not about eliminating fear. It is about learning to evaluate our fears and control their negative powers so that we exhibit courage where courage is needed. Fear can be good and can provide a needed warning. Imagine a person about to walk down a dark alley at night in what is known as a dangerous part of town. A feeling of fear warns him without him having to think about it and, hopefully, persuades him to take another route. Therefore, we do not want to talk thoughtlessly about having no fear. We all want fear to do its designed work of warning us and keeping us from unwanted harm.

Some fears develop without our being conscious of them. They are an instinctive reaction. One of our questions was how we could control these sudden impulses since, at times, they could be so powerful and overwhelm us. Perhaps more to the point were the questions: should we and when can we control these impulses?

These initial surges of emotion that we sometimes call fear may better be described as undefined emotional surges, and they only develop into conscious fear when we decode them and think about them or simply feel them. It is then that we connect them to what is happening in our world, be it the world of our mind or the real world outside ourselves. Whatever the answers to all these questions, we simply wanted to know how to control runaway fear.

We knew that any of us could exaggerate our fears, so learning to analyze the facts that stimulated us to fear would also be helpful. Have you noticed that fears do not always tell you the full truth about the facts? All of us want to operate on the truth and if we were face-to-face with a volcano, we certainly wanted to read the facts correctly.

Something else concerned us about our reactions to fear: we knew we tended to transfer a fear from one object to another without it being a rational transfer. For example, I hate spiders. Now, I know that some are harmless and some, like the brown recluse, are deadly, but all spiders get tarred with the same brush in my mind, at times, creating an irrational transfer of fear from one to the other. Perhaps it is because I simply don't want to make a mistake in my identification. Whatever the reason, generalizing a fear is not rational and we wanted to do better.

The more we thought about it, our irrational generalizing was perhaps not a rational reaction as much as it was a struggle within us with fear that had us in its grasp. Fear was becoming an increasing challenge for us and we were beginning to realize fear resided *within us,* not in the world around us.

The path to confidence is in ousting or in understanding and control of fear, the development of faith, and the ability to sustain beliefs that lead us to self assurance and trust. Even though fear does not completely leave when we focus on our beliefs (we might still feel afraid), faith keeps the negative effects of fear from gaining ground, influencing our decisions, and taking our thoughts captive.

Part of the planning of the expedition that is used in this book to illustrate our ousting of fear included going over all the mental preparations we needed to make. Fear could easily gain the upper hand if we were mentally and emotionally ill-prepared.

When facing a challenging experience, these mental preparations, although often overlooked, are as important as planning the supplies and equipment for an expedition. For example, if you are afraid of losing your job, mental preparation is as important as getting feelers and resumes out in search of another job. Unfortunately, we do the later, not the former, and suffer from fear more than we should.

When contemplating our forthcoming expedition we noticed that fear could begin beforehand, increase as we near the feared event, and last a lifetime if we do nothing about it. Therefore, preparing beforehand to overcome fear's unwanted stranglehold was not only wise but seemed to us needed and achievable. Additionally, we had to think about the afterglow of a fearful event to avoid our minds becoming infused with a chronic fear of all volcanos or of all fearful challenges.

It is hoped that these ideas for mentally preparing to overcome fear will help you be thorough in dealing with fear whenever you need courage and confidence. It may seem like a great deal of work, but the greater the challenge, the more preparation we should commit to it. Make a wise choice regarding the amount of preparation you may need.

First, Identify Your Fear and Name It Accurately

Fear Can't Be Grasped

The ancient Greeks said fear was a god who controlled us. The rugged, fearless Spartans, who earned their reputation for being self-disciplined, tough, and unusually bold, built a temple to Phobos, the god of fear, depicting her as a grotesque, fearsome creature. They were aware of fear's terrifying characteristics. But fear does not have to control us, and you can't grasp or capture a god and control it either. In contrast, we understand that fear is not a god, but a self-generated emotion, and appears wherever there is a lack of faith. We can control it, and we must look inside ourselves to find it and manage it, so first, name it accurately.

Don't just say, "I'm afraid." Afraid of what? Controlling fear can be a very difficult task, because it can induce panic or immobility in a second and if all we do is try to get rid of our unnamed fear, we will most certainly fail. Fear comes in various emotions and there are no handles or grips to seize and remove an emotion. **We must deal with the cause of our fear, not the emotion or what we observe as the symptom.** Success begins in knowing which fear is gripping us to be able to remedy the cause of it.

Ask, "What am I really afraid of? Is it the powerful thrust of the vent (a fear we most certainly felt) that is scaring me, or is it the thought of dying, or perhaps the terror of the unknown?" And we will learn to also ask, "Is the fear within me or in the realities of my circumstances?"

Consider:
If we don't know what we are afraid of, how can we zero in on the right solutions?

Fears come in many forms. Hence the need to identify what fear we are facing. Not all the fears we faced on White Island were the same. Fears of physical danger, lack of mental fortitude, being distracted from keeping our vigilance, concern for our mates, forgetfulness, and more, all showed themselves. We will discuss some of them below.

Remember, THE FIRST TASK IS TO ACCURATELY DEFINE YOUR FEAR.

When Facing Fear

When fear hits, use the tools and the principles for overcoming fear that are presented here or others that you have found effective and...
- Mold them to the particular challenges you face.
- Choose what best fits your temperament
  Remember, whatever tools you master, become familiar with them and use them to prepare yourself for other life challenges you may face in the unknown future. A pilot of an aircraft knows the validity of this diligent practice.

If you do this, you will have a reliable, customized method for building confidence in similar circumstances.

Most of us avoid the small effort this identification requires. Why? What are your avoidance techniques or excuses for? Not identifying your fears. Writing them down will help you address them seriously.

Among our fears on White Island were:

- *The physical danger.* We couldn't do much about that. We knew we would be helpless in the face of a massive eruption that tore the crater apart, or even a pyroclastic surge. The only thing we could control was within us: our thoughts and emotions.
- *The fear of the unknown.* Gain all the knowledge you can in advance and make the best decision you can as you go along. This, again, was all we could do. Keep doing what you know! When we keep doing what we know, we confront what we don't know and the struggle to learn how to handle the unknown increases our knowledge even more.
- *The need for mental fortitude* to keep pressing on in the face of the scary sensations. Our sight, hearing, smell, and touch were all to experience strange and frightening input — the acid droplets that stung and that we couldn't see, for example. Could we remain focused on positive thoughts in the raw face of these unexperienced negatives?
- *Not believing in ourselves.* Would we have sufficient confidence in ourselves since we were inexperienced? Experience buys a great deal of courage. Confidence must buy the rest. Could we gain courage from our faith?

  Handling the internal reactions from a sudden surge of fear that could paralyze us at any moment. Would we freeze and, if so, how would we make ourselves respond? Simple, calm deliberation would not be enough. We had to know ourselves and our likely responses to trouble. We needed, as best we could, to mentally train our impulses and experience those impulses beforehand to develop some kind of positive habitual behavior.

Name your main or typical fears:

_____

_____

_____

_____

_____

Next, Name the Causes and Imagine the Triggers of Fears

What causes fear? Almost anything, even fear itself. Knowing the cause provides us with a target at which to aim. We rehearsed the imagined and known causes of our fears many times and discovered that all causes of fear were within ourselves, not in the physical circumstances around us.

The Causes

The causes were not the sight of the exploding vent, the sting of the acid droplets, the trembling ground, and the thunderous noise, but our response to them. This is a hard lesson to learn, because we want to blame something else, not ourselves, for our fears. All fears are defined by our reactions to people, to our own thoughts, or to our environment. Reactions or responses to outside or inside stimuli are the direct cause of our emotions.

We could control our responses to a degree, but not the actions of the volcano, so "control what can be controlled" became our mantra. Confidence is built by controlling what we can. Beyond that, it is a matter of trust in God for those who have a belief in a divine being, or it is simple acceptance of fate for others.

The Triggers

The triggers for us were anything that caught us by surprise or was more than our senses could handle. Planning well mentally was, again, the only answer to that. Imagine and prepare for every scenario (imagination and intuition are, perhaps, our most amazing mental tools).

Visualization was the method in our days of preparation. Mentally rehearsing our responses to what might trigger fear helped greatly and, yes, we rehearsed in our waking moments at night in the weeks before we left. Positive, vivid imagining of facing a fear and reacting to manage its effects can increase confidence when finally facing the fear.

Staying focused on the goal and the rewards also helped us ward off the negative effect of the triggers that did occur. As mental practice, I imagined being there already, doing all we had to do, and coming back unharmed. I dreamed of the use of the 35 mm slides I would show many times in New Zealand and Australia, the talk I would give, the booklet I would write, and the personal growth from the accomplishment of inner control — a result I treasured most.

We kept asking ourselves, "What is our best response if what happened in the past eruptions happens again?" Focus on that response and see yourself faithfully doing it.

The past is a source of wisdom; the present is where wisdom is forged and fashioned, and imagining the future possibilities is where wisdom is given a trial run. We studied all that we could find that had been written about the island — news articles, scientific papers — and we studied the old photographs. The crater floor changes constantly and when we arrived, it bore no real resemblance to the photographs. So what was the benefit of looking at all those old photographs? Mental preparation and mental practice. Some of the photographs appeared worse than the reality we found, and some didn't prepare us for the scene we met.

How Did Our Minds Work?

Our thoughts either promote or reject our feelings. An emotional reaction to a scary situation is to be expected. That's the way we are wired. However, the wiring is not the same for all of us. For some, the emotions are powerful and overwhelm them. Their emotions are almost as frightening as the frightening situation itself while for others, they are somewhere between a rush of excitement and a kind of temptation to take the dare.

Typically, when you are afraid, what do your thoughts do? Do they follow your feelings of fear and succumb to them, supporting their every call? Or do they argue against your feelings of fear? Are they leading you into fear or warning you against it? Each of us has our own typical way of thinking when it comes to fear. Know thyself!

It's true that most of us don't think of what our thoughts or feelings are doing when we are afraid. We just react in whatever way we feel or think at the moment. A little thought tells us that rational beings need to be more analytical of themselves. Going with the flow, so to speak, is not very creative or helpful. So "what did we typically do" was a mind-opening question.

We reasoned something like this: if our thoughts can be the promoters of our fears — in fact, be the real culprits that escalate it and cause us to panic — we had to identify and change any patterns of thinking that encouraged fear, or we simply become its robot. If our thoughts fought our fearful emotions and called us to face them and control them, then we had to learn how to follow our thoughts.

A New Mind

This called for a renewing of our minds. A man who faced great fear in his life, Paul, once said, "Be transformed by the renewing of your minds." His aim was to think with the courage of God when he faced fear. That's a tall order, but a great aim. He exhibited this ability on a number of occasions and became a model for us. A new mind means new beliefs, and that was certainly what I needed in the face of fear. We had to learn to think with faith and trust, resting in their optimism, comforted by their upward gaze, knowing we have done what we could and that what is out of our control is to be deliberately handed over to faith, not to worry. Here's a good question to ask yourself: Do you hand your fears to faith or worry?

Faith is a way of thinking, among other things. It is a belief in someone or something that is bigger than we are, a belief that calms our minds when we are afraid. We will talk about what that is later.

First, identify and know your typical thought patterns that you could call your "fear thinking." Train yourself not to fall into fearing your own thoughts: afraid of your virtual reality when it hasn't become reality in the outside world yet. If the fear is still only virtual, it is time for calm and reason and careful planning, not for premature panic. If you need to follow your thoughts when afraid, do so.

Try to describe to yourself how you think when you are afraid. What is your typical response to fear? Write it down as best you can. For all of us, this should be informative.

It all came down to the control of our minds, which meant the control of our thoughts. Thoughts can speed up, go blank, turn negative suddenly or freeze. Know what is happening in your mind and be able to describe your inner behavior to yourself and call on your rehearsed solutions and your positive faith-filled thoughts.

Three Mental Processes

You will use three mental processes to gain knowledge of your mental behavior. They are called:

- *Self awareness,* which is a knowledge of what is on the back burner of your mind. These residual thoughts (your mental tone or temperature) can raise or lower your level of anxiety and make fear more or less likely. Cleanse your mind of all negative memories. They do us no good. Allow only positive memories to loiter.

- *Introspection*, which is intentional examination of what you are honestly thinking. We tend to fool ourselves by believing we are thinking positively when we are not. Hence the need for this introspection.
- *Consciousness*, the knowledge of what is on the front burner of the mind and what you are actively processing. Keep your mind on the task. A wandering mind can introduce the unexpected and be attracted easily by fears. Focus actively on whatever creates feelings of productive calm, like faith, love, and success. Always do something about any negative thoughts you discover, because they are the enemy when it comes to overcoming fear.

Face the fears you discover; expose yourself to them in your imagination; live through them positively to strip them of their terror, and successfully manage them in your virtual world. Carry no fears with you; they are too heavy for you.

In the days before the expedition, we rehearsed our mental challenges, building confidence in our minds — confidence that comes from repeated mental exposure to fear with no negative result. Isn't it great that we can do this safely in our minds? Whatever you do, **do not rehearse your unwanted responses.**

So far we have learned:

- To accurately identify our fear
- To name the cause of our fear

- That the causes of all fears are our responses to fearful things or scary thoughts
- To watch for the typical triggers that spark our thoughts of fear
- To watch for the thought patterns that usually result in our turning negative and fearful
- To be aware of what is simmering on the back burner of our minds
- To understand what we are honestly thinking
- To always pay attention to what our thoughts are currently engaged in, because these thoughts can predict the next moment of our lives.

Challenge and Replace Irrational Beliefs

Real, but Irrational, Fears

Even though physical danger is life threatening, it ranks lower than our most common fears, which are the fears of rejection, ridicule, and failure (according to psychologist, Paul A, Hauck). Again, we noted that our worst fears came from within, not without, and were the product of our beliefs. Beliefs need to be accurate and positive, or at least as much so as we can make them.

We needed to name and understand our real fears, not the external catalyst of our fears (physical danger). Remember, our real fear could be fear of failure, pain, death, embarrassment or, simply, the unknown.

Fear of fear also ranks high on the list of human fears, but like fear of rejection, ridicule or failure, it is also unreasonable. Although fear of fear is real, it does not make sense.   Why fear the response (the feeling of fear)? It is better to be realistically related to the stimulus of our fears or to effectively handle the emotions that they produce.   Better to fear getting killed or to fear not adequately handling the fear of being killed than fear the fear of being killed.

Afraid of Ourselves?

Fearing our own emotion puts us in a losing situation mentally. We are actually fearing ourselves. We already said you should not fear your fearful thoughts. Here we are saying, "Don't fear the emotions they generate or the emotion that generated your fearful thoughts in the first place." For that matter, don't fear your emotions or your thoughts. Again, fearing one or both is fear of ourselves and surely that's irrational for rational creatures. We are to overcome the negatives of fear with the powers we, as positive creatures, possess and in which we are designed to function. Most of us have clearly observed that, when we are negative and filled with doubt, we look to others and feel to ourselves very different creatures from when we are operating with the high-octane fuel of faith. Is doubt substandard energy? What do you think?

Most frightening situations aren't dangerous.   Did we believe that? Do you? Had we processed this thought and benefited from it?   Scientists evaluate a volcano's behavior, checking tremors and the volcano's recognizable seismic patterns, and are able to enter volcanos to install detection equipment with a degree of safety. Volcanoes are not totally unpredictable, or so we had to believe. Don't believe that a fear is rational just because you think it represents danger.   Our perception and definition of danger changes when we are afraid. Change your belief to one that introduces the positive world of faith and asks your positive beliefs to examine the situation too.

People were telling us how dangerous it was to go to the island and land on it. "What if...," the fear pundits were shaking their heads at us. When we went, as I indicated, we didn't have the benefit of seismic information or "leveling" of the crater floor or temperature measurements, and we were, in the minds of many of our friends, taking a foolish risk. What facts we did have indicated pauses between eruptions, patterns that were observable that could aid us, and a belief that, risk or no risk, we could make it. It was this latter belief that really made us choose to believe we could complete the expedition — alive. The fear of our fears could not stop us because, to faith, how foolish that sounded.

Other irrational patterns of thought will occur to you, no doubt, and you can strip them of their irrationality too.

First, Understand What the Facts Are

We have mentioned our perception of things. We do not always perceive facts the same way and, sometimes, we have diametrically opposite interpretations of them from other people. Go over the facts, even if you think they are incontrovertible facts and need no reevaluation. Facts can appear to be true when they are only our perception of the truth, a half-truth or a persistent bias we have nurtured.

Each temperament looks at the facts differently. The SPs interpret optimistically; the SJs prefer to err on the side of caution; the NTs, according to the theory they are propounding or adhering to, and the NFs, optimistically if they have chosen to act on a possibility. Whatever our temperament, when we feel we have solid facts to rely on, we always feel more confident. (For an understanding of the reactions of the temperaments in various situations, see *INNERKINETICS* — *Your Blueprint to Excellence and Happiness* by Ray W. Lincoln.)

We found the facts we felt we could rely on. They were:

- How many have died on White Island during its recorded history? Ten or twelve, who foolishly lived on the Island mining sulphur ('foolish' indicates where we drew a limit to our confidence). The names of ten are recorded, yet some say eleven and most, twelve. Why the inconsistency? I was never able to find out. We had no plans to live there or expose ourselves to the dangers any longer than our goals demanded.
- How many expeditions recorded no harm? All but one.
- Does the volcano change its performance suddenly without notice? No — at least not usually. (Notice again where our level of confidence drew a line, accepting the "not usually" as our guide.)
- If we sensed changes in the volcano's behavior, we would leave immediately on the windward side, out of the path of its worst fury. That was our plan and one that could avoid danger — except in a really major eruption, which we believed should give some indication that it was about to happen. We had a well-studied plan, even if it was not foolproof. Perfect plans evade all of us. Our plan was acceptable to our belief levels.
- For those who don't want any risk in life (and that was not us) simply stay away from volcanoes and all

risky happenings.　　And also, incidentally, don't move, since any movement always carries a small degree of risk!

It was a matter of <u>how much</u> risk we were willing to take. In life.　It is always just that!　We carefully named our fears and built what we felt were realistic beliefs about them, assessing the risk we were willing to take.

Second, Interpret the Facts Fairly

Our interpretation of the facts is where most of our fearful thinking takes place.　If a fact horrifies us, we speak about it in horrifying terms.　Self talk is no different.　An emotional reaction can set in and, if we ruminate on it more and more (rumination is self talk), we talk ourselves into the mouth of fear.　A mountain is soon built out of a small hill in a mind that ruminates negatively.

But is it a mountain or a hill?　Is our interpretation fair? Have we colored the facts with our own fearful emotions or thoughts?　To be able to defeat the mounting fear inside of us, we have to retreat to the facts and make as near to an unbiased assessment of them as we can, turning aside the noisy clamber of our fearful emotions and thoughts.　It's in the belief that we are operating on the real, fairly interpreted facts that confidence is built.

Can we do this?　Can we exclude our emotions?　Not really.　All our thoughts are colored with how we feel about them.　　Thoughts arise out of emotions and emotions themselves arise out of memories (among other things) and those memories are colored by our culture and our environment.　　The drives of our temperament have a lot to do with the amount of risk we feel comfortable with.   Therefore, if we can't be completely unbiased, what should we do?

Facts don't always need to be seen without our emotions because, sometimes, emotions are an essential part of the facts. We must make a fair evaluation of them, and that is not always easy to do.   Fear, if it is being evaluated, must not be allowed to speak the loudest in our minds. Faith should be given at least equal time at the podium. And don't forget that our values and core beliefs on which we live our lives should be heard and not violated by our fears.

Another way is to ask a less biased person to help us see the validity or lack of validity in our evaluation. We chose to listen to people who had some knowledge of volcanoes and, aside from what had been written about the Island, those people were hard to find. Our friends were not the experts they thought (and wanted us to think) they were. Counsel is a chief source of wisdom and clear insight. We did not believe we had better minds than others — equal maybe, but not better.

Other Irrational Beliefs

We also believed that setbacks are irrationally seen as indications that we should abort our plan. We had setbacks. Captain after captain refused to take us to the island and wait there till we had finished before they could leave. Most were of the opinion that they would drop us off and come back six or so hours later, if conditions were favorable. Can you imagine that we didn't like that? In the face of difficulties, we believed that these setbacks were a part of progress. One by one, we were eliminating the kind of captain we would not feel comfortable with. Imagine being deep in the heart of the crater and being relayed the message that the captain got cold feet and left!

When fear struck, as it did when we were facing the awesome force of the main vent at close quarters (I keep referring to this moment since it made such an impression on me), I made myself think of the progress we had made.

> We were more than halfway done, with no observable alterations in the volcano's behavior. We were a little less than half a mile from Crater Bay. If we had to make a dash for it, we had at least a chance.

You may think this would be little comfort when we were half a mile away. But it was all we had to cling to in our minds, so we clung to it. Cling to what you have when facing fear.

"Soon we would have gathered all the information we needed and be headed home," is what we told ourselves. Could we stay the course? That was the question to be answered, not some negatively amended version, such as how quickly could we retreat and get off the island. Fear plays havoc with those kind of thoughts.

Fear is real, but the danger may not be as real as the fear. What could happen seemed less urgent than completing our tasks as soon as possible. I also noticed that when I left the main vent and pressed on to the back of the crater, the fear subsided somewhat. When what is stimulating our fears no longer takes center stage in our minds, the fear fades with the change of focus. This is a fact for all who would learn how to master fear.

We learned the following lessons:

- Our fear of physical danger is not our greatest fear
- Fear of fear-filled emotions makes no sense
- We often ruminate on the negative things and not the positive
- Most frightening situations are not dangerous
- The danger is sometimes not as real as the fear
- Understand and interpret the facts clearly
- Facts are not always what they seem
- Emotions are facts and cannot be excluded from our decisions
- The emotion of fear must not be allowed to drown out the arguments of faith
- Setbacks are not proof you should abort your plan
- Keep your mind on your positive beliefs
- In counsel there is wisdom

Name one irrational belief you have about fear.

_____

_____

_____

_____

_____

_____

_____

Develop a Clear Strategy

A strategy deals with contingencies: what ifs, what thens, if this — then what. Foreseeable errors and surprises are the meat of strategies. It only takes a little thought and discussion to think of most contingencies. Plan for all contingencies ahead of time as best you can. Know what you will do in each case. Remember, no plan can thoroughly deal with the impossible or the unknown. It is a logical impossibility.

Next, a strategy needs careful execution. We made careful observations from the first sighting of the island to the landing, and made firm, but flexible, guidelines about all plans to explore the crater. Because only two people went deep into the crater, this was not a gigantic task in planning. The flexible parts of the plan were decided when we faced a decision. As we explored the crater, each action was made with the guidance of our strategy and the input of the moment we faced. We thought this was the best way to execute a plan when there were many unknown variables.

First, a Safe Landing

Plans were made to make a safe landing on the beach, which we had read was composed of rocks, not sand. That's all we knew. Landing was our first experience of having to make an impulsive change to our plans. We had overlooked the fact that the acids from the vents in the crater drained into the ocean, and the water in Crater Bay would be acidic. Fortunately, it was only mild enough to shock us and burn a little, but not enough to harm us as we jumped out of the small boat to steady it and stop it from being dashed on the rocks with each swell. Rubberized waders were donned gladly after that first burn!

Next, Good Communications

The monitoring of the conditions with the captain of the vessel and with me during the expedition were carefully planned as we fanned out to cover a large crater floor. He wanted to know when we would be back and whether he should leave before we got back. (The answer, of course, was NO!) We did wonder if he might lose his nerve and leave without us. We had no communication devices, and calling to each other was out of the question due to the excessive noise, so all the communications were by semaphore or predetermined signals.

Plans had to be adjusted, once more, on the spur of the moment. Clothing that disintegrated in the acidic air, the unexpected need to protect photographic equipment, and the unexpected brilliance due to a bright sun on a white landscape were the main alterations and adaptations and were, in the most part, effectively made.

Plans for who would do what, and who wouldn't, were meticulously followed. For that, everyone was to be thanked.

Plans for constant monitoring of the conditions within the crater walls (swirling winds, changes in the color and sound of escaping gases) and the communication with each other of warning signs, also, proved adequate. If the volcano had not been emitting such a huge column of gas and ash (two to three times the height of the island), these concerns would not have been so urgent. Planning an Escape Procedure

The retreat, if any, was simple; not much planning was needed.

- At a given time and signal, the support party would re-board the boat to make ready for an expeditious departure.
- The exploration party would have to retreat and board via a dingy, one-at-a-time, as they arrived.

Planning Breeds Confidence

All this preparation gave us a confidence that we otherwise would not have had. We are beings created with that a world, our mind, to plan and test run our plans. It is here, in our minds, that we gain or lose confidence. Confidence is lost when our minds turn from positive to negative or when we panic with no plan.

Preparations that spell out the fact that we have learned how we typically react to surprises and what we typically do when faced with fear are preparations for life, not just for a special adventure. In this way, we were conscious we were on a growth curve in all we were doing.

We Learned
- Strategy is not all that hard, just time consuming
- Planning really does increase confidence
- All plans should be flexible enough to accommodate the unforeseen
- It is important in life to plan your exits as well as your entries

- All we do is a preparation for life.

The Challenges of Fear Come in Three Timeframes

Before it Happens

Before we are faced with fearful events, our expectations can run wild and our imagination can either be a tool to control fear or create it. In this phase, faith and belief play a vital role, making us look to ourselves and others like we are made of clay or steel, in the image of fear or faith. Projects, dreams, even the course of our lives can be made or destroyed in this phase. It is here that we either accept or reject possibilities.

Remember all those preparations? Faith, without appropriate works, is dead! But don't underestimate the power of imagination, intuition, expectations, and dreams. And remember: they, in partnership with reason, direct all the planning. Make them all work positively for you as well.

During the Challenge

During the challenge, faith will be tested in the heat of the actual battle with our fears and circumstances. It is here, in the moment of trial, that faith can win over doubt or the lack of it can cause us to give in to failure. Faith, itself, is never the cause of failure. Faith that oscillates with doubt fails, because doubt adulterates the faith, and faith loses its focus.

This is where we perform. Performance is according to our faith. The quality of our actions is never praised if it is fashioned by fear. It even felt good to think this way.

After the Challenge

After the challenge is over, residual fear can make us determined not to face fear again or determined never to let it defeat us. The child that falls off the bike for the first time faces the after-challenge of fear, either to get back on the bike and try again or never to try again.

After we have faced a trial we can increase our dependency on faith or lessen it. Faith must live on in us, gaining a mastery of our lives, instilling one stroke of confidence after another, rising to applaud our positivity, settling in to captain us and reinvigorate our self-discipline. If your faith is rooted in God, add: keeping us supplied with divine sources of power.

Replace Fear with Faith — How?

The Nature of Fear

The Greeks called fear *phobos*. *Phobos* meant terror. But it was used for the whole spectrum of terror: for the kind of fear that paralyzes or demotivates us, alarms or alerts us, the kind that frightens or scares us, even for the feeling of simply being unnerved.

Surprisingly, it was also used for respect: the feeling that has us in awe of something or someone — a reverence that leads us to the experience of worship. Hence, we find *phobos* used as the fear of the gods and, because the word can mean fright or awe, we are left to interpret the experience as either an experience of awe or outright terror with no guidance as to its meaning, except for the context within which we find it.

As we might imagine the word is old and belongs to the Mycenean period (the period of the Trojan War heroes), about the eighth to the sixth century BC. Fear is an emotion we all learn early in life. We soon need a name for this feeling and all peoples reflect that need early in the formation of their language.

The nature of fear is not, as we might suppose, to be scared, but to believe something or someone is, in some way, greater than see are and, therefore, has power over us. As a result, fear is like faith. Both believe something or someone is greater than we are and will have power over us, a power that can hurt or benefit. Faith in something weaker than ourselves makes little sense, since we should be able to control it and that it cannot control us.

We also need to remember that the nature of fear is to control us. It wants to rule our thoughts and our minds. In contrast, we should be in control of ourselves and let our thoughts be taken captive by the highest good. (Here's a good question to probe your beliefs: How do you define the highest good?) Fear is only an issue in our lives when it controls our minds. Otherwise, it is simply background static. We had, that day, the choice of whether fear controlled us or faith controlled us. When it comes to what controls you, it begins with a choice.

Fear leads to anxiety. Fear that is followed by anxiety or fear that creates anxiety is denoted in the biblical literature by the words "fear and trembling" (*phobos kai tromos*). Anxiety is a fear that causes us to physically or mentally tremble, or both. We never read of the phrase "faith and trembling." That's because faith should produce calm, not a nervous panic. If it does not produce calm, we are not yet trusting. Nerves are settled by faith and set on edge by fear.

The middle ground between faith and fear is awe. Hence the Hebrew-Christian understanding of the fear of God as a reverence generated by awe. The use of *phobos* in all of its meanings in the Bible, from being afraid to being in awe, may confuse some, but not, of course, the Greeks, who knew the wide meaning of their own word.

The Gods

Fearing God (or for the Greeks, gods) was not the same for the Hebrews as it was for the Greeks. In the Greek translation of the Hebrew scriptures, the word "fear" is used mainly of fearing God. Both Hebrews and Christians stood before God in a twofold fear:
- Fear: "It is a fearful thing to fall into the hands of a living God," Hebrews 10:31, and
- Love: "Perfect love casts out fear," 1 John 4:18. Jews, along with Christians, worship without feeling a tension in this paradox. The Greeks, on the other hand, were simply afraid of their deities. Awe for them did not result in love, but in fearful obedience.

The Nature of Faith

It is interesting to note that *pietho* (which is used for faith) is the Greek word for "to convince" and, therefore, to trust in what you are convinced about. It is also the name of the goddess of the art of persuasion. *Peitho* (faith) is created by persuading ourselves about something. How do we have faith? It's simple — by persuading ourselves about something.

We must remember, however, this is both a rational and emotional task. Fear, which is emotionally induced, is removed by reason and by replacing fear with another emotion, a positive one — in our case, the passion to fulfill our task. If you want to have faith, recall that fear and faith both accept that something or someone is greater than ourselves and, in this belief with thoughts and actions that match the belief, awe develops into trust and is the beginning of faith.

Don't look for some complicated system to remove fear. Simply persuade yourself or allow yourself to be persuaded. Whatever we are persuaded about, we have faith in

Confidence, like faith, is also a result of persuading ourselves, of reaching a conviction about something. If you want to be confident, allow yourself to be convinced or convince yourself. The path to confidence is the same as the path to faith. Confidence is a manifestation of faith.

To allow yourself to be convinced about someone is to trust him or her. Therefore, a variant meaning of *peitho* is "to trust." Plato said, "I will obey God rather than you," Apologia, 29d. He had persuaded himself that there was a God he needed to obey (hidden in that resolve to obey is the presence of trust) and that the greater force was divine, not human.

Faith is simple and according to the Hebrew and Christian Scriptures and those of some Eastern religions, we live by faith. It is an accurate observation of how we are made to operate. Belief is the principle on which all humans act. We can't have confidence if we don't rely on something or someone or we are not convinced about something or someone. It follows, then, that we don't do anything without faith of some kind.

Therefore, we reasoned that if we were to face fearsome situations, we would malfunction if we didn't have faith. The presence of fear in humans indicates a malfunctioning of their system. The more we thought of it this way, the more we wanted to prove to ourselves that we were people who had learned the lesson of living healthy lives, and that meant having faith in times of testing.

Abraham, on his ascent of Mt. Moriah to sacrifice his son in obedience to God's command, was being tested in like manner. Was he, the father of the faithful, a man who lived by the principle of faith or not? If you have read the story, you know the outcome: he believed and was vindicated. Gandhi's faith was likewise tested as he sought to free a nation by peaceful means, but in the face of increasing military opposition, it seemed as though he had no hope. He remained firm in his convictions and freed a nation from the greatest military power of the day without firing a shot. The test has come to us all in one way or another, and we know whether we have passed or failed the test. If you have failed, you may retake the test.

For many of us, it may be helpful to see fear as a flag, either alerting us to danger or making us aware that we are not functioning as we are made to function. Fear that is alerting us will lead to our being tested. Will we react with fear or faith? Therefore, to function as designed, whenever you are nervous, react with faith and the wisdom of a well-informed faith. Try these steps.

Steps to Take

In order to function with faith and not under the control of fear, here are some essential steps that you can take to make it happen.

- *Perform actions that support your faith.* Eliminate actions that don't support your faith. An action that is taken out of fear will not encourage faith. Act like your faith would tell you to act for it to win.
- *Focus on Faith, not Fear.* Fight fear with focus on a positive plan and keep your focus strong by using your self control. These are tools we are all familiar with. If we believe we can exert control over our thoughts, we can. Here's an insightful quote: "God has not given us the spirit of fear but of ... self control," said Paul, the great theologian. We can all benefit from the use of our self control that keeps us focused on what we are convinced about in order to overcome fear, because the relationship between fear and self control is a dynamic and practical one.
- *Believe in something or someone who has greater power than the something or someone you are fearing.* Believing in someone bigger than ourselves or a principle that transcends our lives calms our fears. If you are convinced and feel confident that you are doing the right thing, then you have no need to fear anything or anyone. This is called the courage of your convictions — your convictions being something bigger than you that you believe in and are committed to. Paul, who I quoted above,

also spoke of gaining confidence by the use of logic when he said, "If God be for us, who can be against us?" Given his presuppositions, his logic is irrefutable and his psychology is practical.

- *The greater the object of our faith, the greater power our faith generates in us.* This is saying the same as the last point but drawing attention to the effect the object of our faith has on our faith. The obvious example is: when we have faith in a person who has greater authority or power than ourselves, we feel stronger. It has a direct affect on our confidence. Also, when we believe in the authority or reliability of the object of our faith (for example, the object of our faith may be evidence of the veracity of the facts we believe or the ability of a person we trust), our confidence doesn't just strengthen, it leaps exponentially, and we may find ourselves suddenly trusting unconditionally. If so, that's natural, the way we have been made.

- *When faced with the unknown, it always comes down to a choice.* We argued that, if we were alert, we could get out of the way of an eruption. The answer to that argument is true and false. We could not prove we could or prove we couldn't. It came down to a choice based on our personal beliefs. We preferred to believe we would have a chance to succeed. The odds were unknown, since what would happen was unknown. So, we had to believe in one or the other. When faced with the unknown, we must make a choice and stick with it if we want to control the fear inside us. Change only if evidence forces you to change and then, with equal confidence, stick to your altered choice.

- *Stay focused on your task.* This, too, requires the exercise of self control. We tried to keep a one-track mind that was riveted at all times on what we were doing and what we were confident about. It was not until we had left and were circling the island to return to Mt. Manganui that we relaxed and reflected as we let our minds wander over all the possibilities we had faced.

- *Remove any personal guilt, because guilt raises our level of concern, which increases our sensitivity to fear.* "Address the cause of all guilt and rectify it" is good advice. Guilt is a relative of fear and whether the guilt is real or only our guilty feelings that are being falsely nurtured, it decreases our self confidence. We must deal with guilt before we can accomplish this next step.

- *Believe in yourself.* Our belief in ourselves sets the upper limit on our performance. If we believe we can, the ceiling on our performance rises to meet our belief: namely, we can. We believed we could pull this expedition off so, with that belief, our confidence rose to encourage our success. Whether your faith is placed in yourself alone or in both God and yourself, the point is the same: fear will run rampant in your life if you don't believe in yourself.

- *Love what you are doing.* Perfect love casts out fear, and we might challenge that statement by asking, "How?" The answer? Faith is embedded in love and is active in every display of love. When we love, we trust; what we trust, we tend to love. Therefore, love casts out fear because of its element of trust (faith). Love whatever you are doing and fear will be minimized. Our love of knowledge and the rewards that the expedition would bring kept fear at a lower level for us.

- *Create a fear of losing your faith.* But be careful of these negative methods of motivation, because they can backfire by centering your focus on the negative — fear — where you don't want it to be.

- *Build trust in the convictions you have come to believe in.* NFs can be afraid of the awesome power of their own feelings. They, in particular, must build a stronger trust in the power of their convictions. (For an understanding of the temperaments in various situations, see *INNERKINETICS* by Ray W. Lincoln.)

On-the-Spot Steps to Overcome Fear and Build Confidence

The battle against fear is not won beforehand or afterwards but in the moment of challenge. Tools — mental or physical — all help us win. Here are the tools, some of which we practiced beforehand in our minds and have already been discussed. We applied them at the moments when fear struck or knocked loudly.

Prayer

Prayer is an amazing tool to increase faith and can only be explored to its maximum benefit with faith. It not only asks for help from a higher source, it conditions us, lifts our spirits, calms us, examines our motives, and builds our faith. There is no more versatile tool to overcome fear if it is rightly performed. Need I say that the right use of prayer is, undoubtedly, with faith, not with fear or an anxious spirit.

If mixed with fear, prayer can be a negative exercise, increasing our anxiety — the opposite of what it should accomplish. Faith, not anxious fear, creates an atmosphere in which prayer can perform its miracles on us, in us, and for us.

Be Careful Not to Overuse Your Strengths

Overuse of caution creates a timid spirit, as does overuse of sensitivity, confidence, and other strengths. Any overuse of a strength creates a weakness and opens the door to rash presumption and impudence, both mistaken forms of confidence. Courage becomes foolishness and caution morphs into immobility of mind and body with overuse.

Overuse of our strengths is caused by overconfidence. We must be confident of our abilities and self worth, but to lose sight of our limitedness is to forget who we are. Healthy inner life is realistic and optimistic, never unrealistic and pessimistic. Boundaries in life must be recognized and observed to contain and channel our strengths properly. In the face of the volcano's raw power, we were kept from overestimating our abilities or our strengths.

Giving Up Is the Only Way to Fail When Overcoming Fears

We all need help to be strong in the face of fear. Condition your mind with the following understandings when in the heat of challenge, and turn them into solid beliefs for living.

- *"Don't give up" is sage advice, if we want to succeed, and applies equally to the building of confidence.* Fears call for retreat, refusing the wisdom of sound reason, turning reason into worry, and rationalizing our worries as wisdom.
- *Be patient.* This is more difficult than not giving up. The French, Latin, and Greek words from which our

English word, patient, comes contain the notion of having to suffer. Being patient is suffering and calls for the guts and determination that all suffering calls for. See the trial and the preparations through.

- *Persistent struggle against our fears weakens them and has the reverse effect on us.* Fear relies on the intensity of the feelings it produces to stay strong. Injections of hope and faith sap fear of its strength slowly, breaking the hold that fearful feelings have on us.

- *Relaxation Techniques — breathing to calm the nervous system — also weakens fear, because it lowers the intensity of fear's emotions, robbing it of full attention.*

When we take the focus away from our fears, we make it easier to stay the course and not give up.

Don't Lose Touch with Your Positive Self Esteem

Fear wants us to lose confidence in ourselves. Confidence in ourselves is a firewall against fear's intrusion. Here are the steps to a strong, positive self esteem when under trial. Follow them.

- *I remember having a strong belief in our success and in our abilities.* We had studied hard and done our homework. Do your diligence and fear has less to cling to and faith has more to nourish its powers.

- *Faith with works — namely, doing all we can — strengthens self esteem and brings faith into focus in the forefront of our minds.* Again, as I have mentioned before, the actions that support our faith strengthen our faith. If we can have faith in a supreme being we have also prepared the way for faith in ourselves.

- *Instead of pursuing your feelings of upset deliberately, pursue a solution to your upset.* Failure to focus on solutions lowers our feelings of self confidence.

- *Think of facing your fear as doing something courageous.* Lift your faith with positive messages and acknowledgements of what you are accomplishing.

Stay Focused on Your Task

Wherever our attention is directed, our energies are focused. This principle of human functioning is critical to understanding how to keep fear at bay. If we allow our focus to wander onto our fears, it increases the hold on our mind with the intent to captivate our thoughts and feelings. We then produce a powerful negative energy and fall under fear's control. Certainly, don't talk about your fears to anyone unless you are seeking counsel. Talking nervously about them only magnifies them. Here is some help to keep focused in the moment of trial.

- *Keep busy.*
- *Concentrate on what you have to do in the present and in the next moment.*
- *Keep your focus positive and on positive goals.* Faith fades in the presence of a negative mind and grows in a positive mind. The reverse is true of fear.
- *Use positive self talk.* Fear interferes with clear decision-making. We had practiced our thoughts to keep focused on making good decisions. Self talk,

like "Keep calm. It's the only way to make good decisions," or "There has to be a way out of this, just find it," helps.

- *Hide your feelings, not just your thoughts of fear, and don't share them with others.* Fear is contagious. Don't talk "fear talk" to others about the next thing you have to do. If you talk about your fear, you give it wings. The next moment may then be the winning moment for fear.

- *We talked about not confusing problem solving with worrying.* Problem solving is positive in nature; worrying is negative in nature.

These simple things are very hard to do for some people. Struggle to do them anyway.

Defeat Fears — One Step at a Time

Boldness does not have to be a sudden burst of confidence; it can be gradually displayed. Fear is a potent emotion and when we strategize our attempts to attack it and overcome step-by-step, we increase our chances of success.

- *Dissolve fears little by little, if they prove to be too big to handle all at once.* As kids, we approached our first animal carefully, reaching out to touch, and then slowly getting closer. The principle works for all fears.

- *When facing fears, they are likely to get worse before they get better, because you are facing them down.* Therefore, expect it, and don't be fazed by it. But don't forget to keep your focus on your positive beliefs.

- *Stop the talk that makes mountains out of molehills (catastrophizing).* Worry exaggerates emotions of fear. Tell yourself that a situation is terrible, and you will begin to believe and feel it is. Courage is stimulated by confident self talk.

- *Leave or turn away from the source of your fear for a moment and compose yourself if the sights or sounds are over-stimulating.*

- *Use the power of positive visualization.* Talk yourself through the event or the likely happening. Build strength by mental practice and positive self talk.

Don't Try to Remove the Feeling of Fear Altogether

You don't need to remove the feeling of fear completely. Weaken it, and you have won. If a fear has got hold of you, reduce it to accomplishable steps.

Here are some guidelines:

- *Simply try to lessen it.* Trying to remove it all at once is nigh impossible at times, but is what most of us concentrate on.

- *Concentrate on the next positive response to the situation, not on the feeling of fear, and the fear will begin to subside.* Ask,"What is the best positive response I can make to this happening?"

- *Concentrate, also, on calming it and making it manageable.* That's the first goal for all successful emotional control efforts.

We found a very unusual vent, raised about six feet above the surrounding crater floor. To get to its rim and peer into it meant slithering on our stomachs up the slippery volcanic mud that the vent had, no doubt, ejected. I was volunteered! When I reached the rim, I was met with a crater about 50 feet across and about 30 feet deep, but the vent delivered a scare for someone like me, who was already conditioned to the danger the volcano presented.

In the vertical side wall was a jagged hole, about 12 feet high and 3 to 5 feet across that suddenly pumped out toxic gases with frightening power and, at the same time, to my startled gaze, the floor of the vent leapt up about 12 feet and, just as quickly, subsided. Lying on my stomach, camera in hand, with my head peering over the edge, I nearly had a heart attack. Before the vent did anything else I wanted to get a shot of the hole and get out of there — fast. I felt the panic, but I can clearly recall my fear was frozen while I fumbled with the camera, which, all of a sudden, I had forgotten how to use. Having to concentrate on what to do to operate it had banished to the back of my mind the panic I had just felt. A greater positive fear — of not getting a shot of this abnormal vent — banished the fear of what the vent would do next. Concentrate on what you came to do, and you will control the fear that has panicked you.

The Decision of the Moment

Please note that, where possible, we react best to moments of fear when we have done some preparation, either mental or physical. However, it is not always possible to prepare and on-the-spot decisions and actions are what we face most of the time. Since we faced having to make sudden decisions in the crater, we needed the following understanding of how we are made.

Fight or Flight — Which? That's the Question of the Moment

We were created with a mechanism for our protection that also teaches us how we are made to handle fear. When faced with a fear outside of us or one that is only inside our minds (created by our thoughts alone), our human system goes into its fight or flight mode automatically.

- *Palms become sweaty; muscles are primed; the heart speeds up; breathing is deeper; mouths gape; eyes dilate; we lose color; goose bumps appear; all our senses are placed on alert, and we brace for action. Some faint! (Not to be encouraged!)*
- *Then we are faced with the decision of the moment: fight or flee — which?* Being automatically presented with the fight or flee alternatives does not let us off the hook; we must choose. Life is made up of choices, and this is a major moment of decision that must not be taken away from us.

Damage?

The activation of our fight or flight mode is teaching us that we have a part in protecting ourselves from the damaging affects of fear, making the decision to fight or flee. Stress is high in these moments, and the effects of stress can cause our bodies much harm. But, more importantly, it damages our spirit and weakens our determination in the face of future fears.

We know from science how our bodies are weakened by the physiological burden and wear of the stress hormones. Little, however, is said about the weakening or strengthening of our spirits. That is just as important, perhaps even more so. Strengthening is achieved by fighting; and weakening, by fleeing from the fear and not facing it. Because fleeing can weaken our spirit, we should not flee too often. Had signs of stronger volcanic activity appeared to us, we would most certainly have fled. Fighting or facing and working through our fears is by far the most recommended reaction, since building inner strength and an unflinching determination in the face of our fears is investing in ourselves and in our future.

Fear itself does not do us harm. It is our reaction to it that determines whether we harm ourselves or strengthen our spirits.

Teaching?

If we pay attention to our fight or flight system and its warnings, we learn awareness. Therefore, it is a teacher. Awareness is essential, because the reactions of our system are dependent upon it. Know you are afraid. Recognize fear! Most people can do with greater awareness. Start here.

It is puzzling to me how some people, when transfixed with fear, don't recognize that fear has overtaken them.

They are so focused on their fear they can't define it to themselves. In this condition, they learn nothing.

Our fight or flight system also teaches us the need of making a decision, as we have noted, and with it, we are taught (if we learn) that shaping our inner selves is often done by how we act. Our actions shape our minds as well as our minds shape our actions. We must lose sight of neither if we are to grow to our potential. All ethical treatises rely on changing people by pointing them to the right actions, meaning our actions will change our minds. The ancient wise man of Proverbs pointed to the other inbuilt method of change by saying, "As a man thinks, so is he," or so he becomes. Both will be needed in overcoming our fear.

The Words Tell a Story

Our English word for fear tells half the story. It means to terrify or be terrified and comes from an Aryan root that means "to go through." To go through is to face our fear — to fight, working our way through it — and this, as I have indicated, is the best half of the story that the words tell.

Are fears also our teachers? Do we need them to make us into courageous creatures? Life's experiences produce the evidence of what we need to develop in a healthy manner and what we don't need to be able to live successfully. Is life saying to us that fear and trouble are challenges to test and advance us toward our designed potential? I think the evidence from life's experiences suggests that when we react well to its challenges, we do become braver, nobler beings. The answer is, yes. Therefore, we need trials to make us, shape us, and develop the raw potential of our humanity. So plan to go through your trials, fighting your way to a stronger you, and don't try to avoid them all the time.

The Greek word *phobeomai*, the verb form of *phobos*, is less brave than the English word. It means to flee — the other half of the story. Fleeing, removing ourselves from the fearful scene, is sometimes the best reaction but should never become our default mechanism as it has become in most of us. Fleeing can encourage cowardice. It is the easy way out and often forces us to accept humiliation that weakens our sense of value, lessens our ability to endure hardship and challenge, and lowers our estimate of ourselves, all the time diminishing our worth in this world.

Always a Choice

Therefore, after we become aware of fear we have a choice: we can face our fears or run from them. As I have said many times: life is all about making the right choices. We should know when to run and when to fight and if we don't know which, fight. Run only as a last resort. In Colorado we have mountain lions and there are signs that tell us to fight back if we are attacked. It's better to resist being eaten than to try to enjoy it. All Coloradans know this!

When we face a fearful situation without time for preparation, our reflexes and our general conditioning to face fear constructively and confidently are going to be tested. The first test is: will we fight or run? Then our mental toughness will be tested. Can we stay the course and work all the way through our fears?

Part of the reason (an unconscious tug at our hearts at first) for the expedition was to build greater confidence into our lives. The more I thought about fear, the more it became apparent to me that fear had its purpose when we reacted properly. When the moment hits, we will know how ready we are to conquer fear, but not before. Therefore, practice and welcome the test and the trouble that gives you opportunity to strengthen your mental powers.

Afterwards, What?

Reward Success

Look forward to a reward, maybe a celebration. Reward is an essential buttressing of the learning curve. It is a moment of recall, a celebration that sears into our mental pathways the lessons we have learned or the inspiration of our accomplishments. I have recalled my interaction with this volcano many times over the years for this very reason.

White Island stands out as a moment in my life that taught me to be more courageous and work my way through the tough times, and I am very thankful for it. Lying on my desk is a pad with the words of Dr. Robert Schuller, "Tough times never last, but tough people do." The fears, the nervousness, and the struggles toughened me. I hope to remember White Island's lessons of building confidence the next time a tough period in my life strikes.

Do you think rewards and celebrations are unnecessary? As a child, I was taught to be good for nothing. Excuse the pun. Rewards were regarded as unnecessary and a sign of weakness if they were requested. It has been a hard task to shake off the feeling that rewards are superfluous, but now, more and more, I use rewards to celebrate my accomplishments and I view them just as necessary as the celebration of birthdays. A birthday teaches that we should value our lives, and celebrating something we achieved to better ourselves is no less worthy of remembrance. Rewards can also speed our learning, because they inject into the memory pleasant emotions related to learning that make learning a like instead of a dislike.

Plan Your Celebrations

Make it happen as soon after a successful event as you can. I can remember how I studied the landscape of the island for every last detail, trying to fuse them all into my memory forever as we circled the island on the return journey, saying goodbye to one of this world's most intriguing places. Then, as it faded into the distance, the pent-up feelings of ousting fear and wrenching a victory from its grip were at last released and my mind was flooded with worthy, pleasurable feelings as powerful as any fear that had surged into my consciousness when standing before the terrifying force of the main vent. My celebration had begun, private and hidden from others, but nonetheless intense and real — to me a treasured memory that has never been far from my consciousness. It was pausing to reflect that started the inner celebration.

Decide How You Are Going to Write Your Memories?

Most people never think of this; some never heard of it. They just let their memories of important events be recorded with whatever was the dominant feeling of the moment and are content to tuck it away in their memory's attic. If they recall the memory, it is limited to "I felt hurt, or helped, or good, or bad." No thought is given to the fact that they may have filed it away in the company of a negative emotion.

There is a lasting result from any traumatic experience and it can be life-changing for better or worse. I can't remember anyone telling me when I was young and more impressionable, "Now, listen. It is important to remember all frightening events positively, not negatively, for the good they can teach you. So keep repeating what it was about them that, when applied, will make your life better." That would have done me a world of good. Recall the confidence more than the fear. That was the lesson we all needed to learn afterwards.

The Amygdala and Our Spirit

The hot spot of our emotional memories, the amygdala, is key to the learning and memory of fear. If we allow our memory of a fearful experience to retain a negative impact on us, it will shape our future reactions into a fear of fear and every time we face a scary situation, we will be conditioned to flee or tremble. Our spirits will be the weaker for the experience, not stronger. We mentioned the weakening of our spirits by choosing to flee decisions instead of facing them with a firm resolve to work through them. We now know we can weaken our spirits by leaving a negative feeling in charge of our memories.

The neocortex, our rational and analytical brain, is helpful in writing memories that will strengthen us for the future. We can activate its help by analyzing in retrospect the event that has frightened us and finding the positive benefit that will lift our spirits. We can then repeat that benefit to ourselves every time we recall the event, and it will build our confidence and faith more at every recall. We can then turn the lesson into a belief about ourselves and equip ourselves to have positive performances in reaction to fear in the future.

Had we failed to explore all of the crater because fear overtook us, and had we left with the task half done, we could recall the event as a step toward our conquering fear, not as a failure we regretted. Our mental toughness is built by *our* perception of our successes and failures, not on someone else's assessments of them.

Rewriting Damaging Scripts

The neocortex can reinterpret and rewrite the fears we have experienced, but it can't keep the amygdala from reacting to new fears. However, the encouraging news is that we can change our lives — no matter what we have done or not done — with the memories of our past. We can unlearn the fears that overwhelmed us by rewriting the memory, and the memory is never too old to be rewritten.

Emotional Rewriting Is Lifelong

How many memories have you filed away that have negative feelings as their dominant lesson — feelings that have conditioned you to fear certain things? More than you like to think about?

Relearning or rewriting these negative memories, says Daniel Goleman in his book, *Emotional Intelligence*, is not only possible but a Godsend for those who are negatively shaped by past memories. Emotions keep changing as our faith builds or our fear rises. They do not remain static, so take advantage of this knowledge.

Memories are fused into our minds by emotion. The greater the emotional content of a memory, the stronger the memory of the event. If something really scared us, we remember it vividly and in detail. Whenever we face something that contains a similar emotion, we react automatically with intense fear. For a long time, science told us these memories were unchangeable and we were wired this way by our experiences in our memories for the rest of our lives. The adult brain was not viewed as plastic. But as with much we are told, even by science, further discoveries reverse previous knowledge. We <u>can</u> rewrite our feelings and our memories.   We are not doomed with the fears of the past.

Here is a method to rewrite your fears and turn them into positive memories.   It is simple and can be learned by anyone who will take the effort to repeat it enough times and create another memory to store in its place.

Seven Steps to Unlearn a Fear and Create a Positive Memory:

1. *Recall the memory that has created a fear in you.* It doesn't matter what it is or what it is about.   Sit quietly and bring it back to memory.

2. *Think about it thoroughly and find a positive lesson or feeling that you can take from it and that will help you rewrite it in this new light.*   For it to further impact your mind, write this new understanding down.

3. *Reconstruct and relive the story around this positive uplifting lesson.*   Relive it vividly and in a positive way, with positive outcomes that produce positive courageous feelings.   Creating new feelings about the event is the key.

4. Be thankful for this new insight and for the event that taught you this lesson, and repeat your feelings of thankfulness often enough to remember the event for its benefits, not its negative impact, for its positive feelings and not its negative feelings.

5. Tell people of its positive benefits for you. This action of telling others is important.

6. See your life as changed importantly by this event. (This is called visualization.) Remake its outcome in your mind (your virtual world) and remember, your mind does not know the difference between what is lived as a virtual reality as opposed to what is lived in the real world outside your mind.

7. Repeat steps four and six as often as is needed to rewrite your memory so that, when you recall it this way, you will think about it positively.

As an example, here are two ways we could have remembered White Island.

- We could have remembered the terrifying feelings we had about it and how scared we felt. If we did, we would have reinforced the feelings of fear and logged it into our memories as a good reason to be scared of future fears and to make us avoid them. We would have become more fearful generally.

- We chose to remember the feelings of achievement and the feelings of triumph at our success and the courage that welled up in us when we thought about White Island.

A possible explanation for this ability to rewrite our memories may be found in Daniel Siegel's book, The Mindful Brain. On page 43, he explains that modulating a fear may be the result of GABA, an inhibitory neurotransmitter, being released in our brains and affecting the amygdala. The release of this chemical is not the primal cause of the control of our fears, however. If it were, we would be reliant on our brains remembering to release it when it should be released, which is not our human experience. Our experiences tell us we can control the modulation of our fears by deciding to do something about them, which suggests we can control the release of the chemical if desired. What this all means, we do not yet know for certain. What we do know is we can change our minds, brains, and ourselves, so go ahead and use this knowledge of our brain's plasticity and take control.

What we do after our frightening experiences is, perhaps, as important as what we do when we are faced with a fear. Be thankful for the way we are made and explore the potential of creating a fearless life.

Dealing with Anxiety Before, During, or After

The following is an outline of how we can reduce anxiety and may also be helpful in reducing post-traumatic anxiety. We used most of these tools before, during, and after our expedition. Anxiety can well up after an event and turn into a nightmarish experience.

Regain a sense of calm over your emotions by the use of:

- Distraction
- Humor
- Aerobic exercise

- Meditation or prayer (Don't focus on your anxiety when you pray; focus on optimistic thoughts; replay your belief in God's protection.)
- Breathing that relaxes and calms you
- Write or talk to someone about something else to create another focus.

Final Thoughts

I want to be fearless. I feel the downward pull of pessimism each time I let fear control my emotions. To be courageous is to open up the possibilities of life to vaster, more exciting vistas.

Whatever our temperament, a life of confidence and courage is possible. SJs will always be cautious, but they can be cautious adventurers and that's how they like it. NFs are depressed by the appearance of dark clouds on their horizon, but hope, imagination, and faith is their path to living in the excitement of new opportunities and it doesn't take much to make them fall in love with this kind of life. NTs are hopeful and only downcast when they prove, in their own estimation, to be unsuccessful and fail to reach their well-planned goals. NTs love the feeling of adventure as they apply their minds to making all things new and this is life for them. SPs thrill to challenges and know that courage and fearlessness is the only way to live — for them, at least. Opportunists and optimists to the core, if fear dominates the SP, something is sadly amiss. (For an understanding of the reactions of the temperaments in various situations, see *INNERKINETICS — Your Blueprint to Excellence and Happiness* by Ray W. Lincoln.)

Fashion your life with faith, hope, and confidence. It is the path I seek to tread, and it has rewarded me. And please don't forget: go back to the section on "Afterwards, What?" and create your own celebration of your victories over fear.

White Island, you have given me a treasure, an increased feeling of power, a courage, a self esteem, a confidence no currency can buy, and I will not forget your benefits.

About the Author

Ray W. Lincoln is the bestselling author of *I'M a KEEPER* and *INNERKINETICS* and is the founder of Ray W. Lincoln & Associates. Ray is a professional life coach and an expert in human nature. His 40 plus years of experience in speaking, teaching, and counseling began in New Zealand and have carried him to Australia and the United States. He speaks with energy and enthusiasm before large and small audiences.

It was not by accident that he became the international speaker and coach that he is today and acquired the ability to guide so many to a happier, healthier, more fulfilled life. Ray has studied extensively in the fields of Philosophy, Temperament Psychology, and Personology.

A member of the National Speakers Association, his expertise has been used as a lecturer and professor, teacher and keynote speaker, seminar presenter, counselor, and coach. He teaches and leads in staff trainings, university student retreats, and parenting and educational classes as well as other seminars and training events. He also trains and mentors teachers and other professionals and executives — all with the goal of understanding their own temperaments and those of others.

Ray lives with his wife, Mary Jo, in Littleton, Colorado where they enjoy hiking, snowshoeing, fly fishing, and all the beauty the Rocky Mountains offer. Both are highly involved in Ray W. Lincoln & Associates, which they feel is the most important and most fulfilling work of their entire career lives. Each of them fills their own roles (according to their InnerKinetics®) as they travel to speak to groups and to present seminars and workshops throughout the US.

Ray W. Lincoln & Associates

Discover the direction your life is intended to go.

OUR SERVICES INCLUDE

Professional Life Coaching

Educational Seminars and Training

Keynote Addresses

Educational Materials

Free Monthly Newsletter

WATCH FOR THESE BOOKS AND EBOOKS
BY RAY W. LINCOLN

I May Frustrate You, But I'm a Keeper!
(Parenting the Temperaments with Love and Confidence)

INNERKINETICS
(Your Blueprint to Excellence and Happiness)

Intelligently Emotional
(Temperament — Completing the EQ Puzzle)

How to Handle the Anger of Hurt
(Coming in 2013)

At our website, **http://www.raywlincoln.com**, you can:

✓Sign up for our FREE monthly newsletter, which entitles you to receive 15% off all purchases at www.imakeeperkid.com and www.raywlincoln.com.

✓Receive a FREE .pdf download of helpful tools to determine your temperament and the temperament of your child(ren)

✓Find more helpful resources as well as information about our services.

✓Register for seminars and events

My Plan to Overcome My Fear of

_____